# Leonard Bernstein:

## America's Maestro

with a message from
**Isaac Stern**

Written by
**Kenneth M. Deitch**

Illustrated by
**Sheila Foley**

11 October 1992

For Taylor,
Miya, and Kenzie

with best
wishes and
the hope
that you
enjoy
the book.

Kenneth M. Deitch

NEW YORK
PHILHARMONIC

Tanglewood

**Discovery Enterprises, Ltd., Lowell, Massachusetts**

© Discovery Enterprises, Ltd., 1991

ISBN 1-878668-03-X hard cover/library edition; 1-878668-07-2 paperback
Library of Congress Catalog Card Number 91-70821

10   9   8   7   6   5   4   3   2   1

*Printed in the United States of America*

## A Word on the Literature

Burton Bernstein, Leonard Bernstein's brother, has written a beautiful history: *Family Matters: Sam, Jennie, and the Kids.* It is mentioned more fully on page 6. Several other fine books are: John Briggs, *Leonard Bernstein: The Man, His Work, and His World* (1961); David Ewen, *Leonard Bernstein: A Biography for Young People* (1967); Paul Robinson, *Bernstein* (1982); Peter Gradenwitz, *The Infinite Variety of a Musician* (1987). Robinson and Gradenwitz both include substantial discussion of Bernstein's music. Shirley Bernstein did an interesting book about her illustrious brother for young people: *Making Music: Leonard Bernstein* (1963). A comprehensive and excellently documented account of the New York Philharmonic and Bernstein's tenure with it is: Howard Shanet, *Philharmonic: A History of New York's Orchestra* (1975). On Tanglewood, see Herbert Kupferberg, *Tanglewood* (1976) and Andrew L. Pincus, *Scenes from Tanglewood* (1989), both of which are well done. A lively and informative book by someone who spent an important portion of his distinguished career working closely with Bernstein is: Schuyler Chapin. *Musical Chairs: A Life in the Arts* (1977). Leonard Bernstein's own books are: *The Joy of Music* (1959); *The Infinite Variety of Music* (1966); *Leonard Bernstein's Young People's Concerts* (Revised and expanded edition, 1970); *The Unanswered Question: Six Lectures at Harvard* (1976); and *Findings* (1982). *Findings* contains a number of his writings, has a more general orientation than the others, and is, in spirit, somewhat autobiographical. Discovery Enterprises, Ltd. gratefully acknowledges the assistance of the New York Philharmonic Archives, the John F. Kennedy Center for the Performing Arts, The Curtis Institute of Music, Carnegie Hall Archives, The Israel Philharmonic Orchestra, and the Boston Symphony Orchestra in the research of this book.

## Credits

### For photographs from which artwork is derived:

Front jacket (hardcover) and front cover (paperback), Ramon Scavelli; pp. 3 and 30, ICM Artists, Ltd.; family members on pp. 6, 29, and 38, Bernstein Family Collection; p. 8, American Truck Historical Society; p. 18, The Curtis Institute of Music and The Pittsburgh Symphony Society; p. 20, Howard S. Babbitt; p. 22, Carnegie Hall Archives; p. 24, Amberson Enterprises; pp. 26-27, The Israel Philharmonic Orchestra; p. 32, Fred Fehl; p. 40, The John F. Kennedy Center for the Performing Arts; p. 46, Andreas Meyer-Schwickerath; p. 48, Steve J. Sherman; back of jacket (hardcover) and back cover (paperback), Siegfried Lauterwasser.

### For insignia on title page (clockwise, from top left):

Boston Latin School; Harvard University; The Curtis Institute of Music; Boston Symphony Orchestra; The Israel Philharmonic Orchestra; New York Philharmonic.

### For production:

*Book design:* Jeffrey Pollock. *Typography:* Nancy Myers. *Production:* Phyllis Dougherty.

## Subject Reference Guide

Bernstein, Leonard – Biography   •   Musician – Biography
New York Philharmonic – Conductor   •   Tanglewood/Boston Symphony Orchestra.

## Acknowledgments

Many people helped in the preparation of this book, and we thank them all. The following helped in especially significant ways, and we are very grateful: Evelyn Abrahams, Burton Bernstein, Alexander Bock, Jacques Boublis, Stephen Boyd, Schuyler G. Chapin, Morton L. Deitch, Ann E. Diebold, Dwayne Eidens, Wendy Elliman, Paul H. Epstein, Mrs. Oscar Feinsilver, Robert Fleming, Irwin Gittleman, Eric A. Gordon, Robert F. Hannan, Barbara Haws, Alan Heimert, Marvin Hightower, Samuel Penchas, Peter Rosen, Patricia Schwartz, Amy Silveira, Daniel Smith, Matilda Smith, Avi Shoshani, Lisa Sullivan, David Thomas, Christopher Willard.

Isaac Stern

On the following pages you will see and read about Leonard Bernstein's young years and, later, some of the historical moments in a meteoric career that spanned continents.

As a creator he was astonishingly versatile, writing with captivating vitality for the symphony orchestra, theater, ballet, television and film. In each form he was idiomatic but always personal. The sound of a Bernstein phrase and rhythmic thrust was recognizable and remembered.

One cannot explain how so much talent came together in one man. But I knew well his insatiable appetite for words, for ideas, for the logic behind thoughts, and the joy in finding hidden streams of intuitive beauty in the creativity of others. He had a passion for knowledge, and reveled in sharing it with young friends—and many not so young.

It was this necessity to share his passions that infused his conducting, his writing, his speaking. It was part of his warm friendship as was his unending loyalty to his lifelong friends.

He leaves us a clear lesson—have faith in the strength and beauty of the informed mind. Always search for more knowledge, never settling for being comfortably unchallenged. Above all, faith—faith in humanity.

*Dawn of a new life in America for immigrants arriving from the Old World, early twentieth century*

# Origins

hen Leonard Bernstein's parents were married in the fall of 1917, in an unusual way his father was just about marrying the girl next door. Both his father and his mother had been born in Russia. Starting out from nearby places, a few years apart, both had come to America at an early age. They were part of a sweeping migration of Russian Jews trying to escape discrimination, including treatment that was often brutal, and longing to begin a new life in the land called the Golden Country.

Charna Resnick was from Shepetovka, a city in the western part of Russia. Only a day's walk from Shepetovka was the *shtetl* — a Yiddish word for village — called Beresdiv. Beresdiv was home to Shmuel Yosef Bernstein.

In 1905, when she was seven, Charna left home with her mother, sister, brother, and a young male cousin and travelled to America, where her father was already living in Lawrence, Massachusetts. A few years later, in 1908, at the age of sixteen, Shmuel Yosef also set out for America, alone. He was hopeful, but he was also frightened.

Charna and Shmuel Yosef both arrived at Ellis Island. Located in New York's harbor, within sight of the Statue of Liberty, Ellis Island was the main place where immigrants entered America. It was customary for officials at Ellis Island to give immigrants ''American'' names. There, upon her arrival, Charna became Jennie. There, too, Shmuel Yosef became Samuel Joseph.

Life in America provided immigrants certain opportunities, but they did not come easily. Jennie began to work in a textile mill in Lawrence when she was only twelve. For his part, Sam went right to work in New York's Fulton Fish Market. It left him time to attend synagogue and to get a little recreation. The rest was just hard, hard work.

Sam was intent upon improving his lot. He saved every penny possible. When a chance arrived in the spring of 1912 to move to Hartford and work in his uncle's barbershop, he took it gladly. A while later he joined a beauty-supplies business in Boston. Although hired as a stockboy, he understood that there were good prospects for promotion.

By the fall of 1916, Sam was living in Chelsea, just north of Boston. He had a good job and had saved some money. One Sunday a friend invited Sam to join him on a trip by trolley to Lawrence, about twenty-five miles away, where he was going to visit some cousins named Resnick. It was there that Sam met Jennie.

Sam was ready to marry and, before long, was eager to marry Jennie. Although Jennie was wavering, Pearl, her mother, was enthusiastic. She liked Sam for Jennie and wanted the marriage. When Sam bought an engagement ring, he entrusted it to Pearl. Pearl had one of Jennie's sisters slip the ring onto Jennie's finger during the night, while she was sleeping. When she awoke in the morning, wavering or not, Jennie was engaged.

On October 28, 1917, in a small synagogue in Lawrence, in a ceremony performed by an Orthodox rabbi, Samuel Joseph Bernstein and Jennie Resnick were married.

Lenny and Shirley - 1933

Newton House

Burtie - 1935

Sam and Jennie's engagement - 1917

Sharon House

*Illustrations of family based on photos from the Bernstein Family Collection. A source of much of the information about Bernstein's early life in this book is a two-part series that appeared in* The New Yorker *on March 22 and 29, 1982. (© Burton Bernstein) It was subsequently published as a book:* Family Matters: Sam, Jennie, and the Kids *(Summit Books, 1982) © Burton Bernstein.*

# Childhood and Youth

eonard Bernstein was born on August 25, 1918, in Lawrence. He was at first named Louis, but there was already a Louis in the Resnick household — his young uncle. To avoid confusion, he soon became known as Leonard and called Lenny. In time his name was formally changed.

Lenny had problems with his health right from the start. He had asthma. "When he was a sickly little boy and he'd turn blue from his asthma, Sam and I were scared to death," Jennie has said. "Every time he had an attack, we thought he was going to die. I would be up all night with steam kettles and hot towels, helping him to breathe." He was plagued not only by these struggles with asthma but also by frequent colds and attacks of bronchitis.

Eventually the family grew to include three children. Lenny was five when Shirley Anne was born and thirteen when his brother Burton arrived.

In the Bernstein household, Sam was the central and dominant figure. Judaism was precious to him. He had been raised as an Chasidic Jew; Chasidism is an especially devout branch of the religion. Burton remembers him as an "Old Testament figure," and Sam always remained deeply interested in the Talmud. His own father had been a scholar-rabbi, and if Sam had not come to America, he might well have followed the same calling.

During Sunday dinner, conversation tended to turn to Jewish subjects of a serious nature, although sometimes it would take an amusing twist. Sam once referred to Dwight Eisenhower as "General Eisenberg" and called Adlai Stevenson "Steve Adelson."

In modern America, it was hard not to make some compromises with devout Judaism. One the Bernsteins made came in the area of food. At home, food was strictly kosher. Away from home, all restrictions were off.

Although Sam did not put a career as a scholar-rabbi totally out of his mind upon arriving in America, he chose a career in business instead. When the moment felt right, he gave up his steady job and started his own firm, the Samuel Bernstein Hair Company. It was around the time of Shirley's birth.

Things were not so easy at first, but a few years later Sam acted on a hunch that turned out to be a good one. He won the New England franchise for an improved version of a device called the Frederics Permanent Wave Machine, and it quickly became very popular. As Sam recalled it: "One day in 1927 I didn't have a nickel to my name. The next morning I went into my office and it looked like every salon operator in New England wanted a Frederics.... I suddenly had money in the bank, credit everywhere, a name for myself.... It was what you call the American dream coming true." Before long he had fifty employees.

Within the Boston area, Brookline and Newton were the most popular places for a prospering Jewish family to live, and in 1933 the Bernsteins moved into their own home in Newton. After having lived for years in a succession of apartments, Jennie was delighted. Around the same time, the family also acquired a summer house in Sharon, about twenty miles south of Boston.

Lenny's first piano arrived when he was ten.

From a young age Lenny showed an imaginative, creative spirit. One sign of it emerged when he was ten. Prompted by their studies of the Roman republic in grammar school, he and his best friend, Eddie Ryack, founded a new nation. They named it Rybernia. It had a language called Rybernian, requirements for citizenship, and even a national anthem. Shirley gained her citizenship right away. Burtie, who had not even been born at the founding, gained his in due course. For the three Bernstein children, Rybernia became a wonderful world of their own. And it endured. Well into adulthood they would still retreat into it, speaking the language and delighting in the very special feeling of closeness it gave them.

Schooling for Lenny did not just mean attending the regular elementary school. He also attended Hebrew school which provided a course of study culminating, when he was thirteen, in his bar mitzvah at Temple Mishkan Tefila.

His studies in Hebrew school had produced some interesting moments much earlier. When he was seven he was transferred from Miss Yeslawsky's class to Miss Gans' more advanced one. Miss Gans also handled dramatics. During rehearsals Lenny would sometimes try to play the piano at moments when Miss Gans did not welcome his creative effort, and she would shout over to him: "Get away from that piano, Leonard Bernstein, and stop banging!" But she also discovered that he had musical talent, and she soon stepped aside and allowed him to lead the singing.

Still, during Lenny's early years, music had entered his life in only a very minor way. Then one day, when he was ten, the situation changed totally. The Bernsteins were living in their apartment on Schuyler Street in a section of Boston known as Roxbury. Aunt Clara, Sam's sister, was moving to New York and decided to leave her upright piano with her brother. Once Lenny gained access to that piano, he became mesmerized by music. He started to experiment on his own, and soon he was begging for lessons.

Frieda Karp, a young neighbor, was a piano teacher. Lenny began studying with her for a dollar a lesson. He learned quickly. After about a year he was playing, if not more skillfully than Frieda, at least more vigorously, and he was ready to advance. On his own, he went to the New England Conservatory and made arrangements to study with a teacher named Susan Williams. Each lesson cost him three dollars.

Lenny's course of study with Miss Williams went on for several years, and in fact, it probably lasted too long because she insisted on an odd technique for positioning his fingers that, as he progressed, became noticeably more of a hindrance than a help. In all events, it was time to move on once more, and Lenny sought out Heinrich Gebhard. By reputation, he was Boston's leading teacher, and he was also a distinguished concert pianist.

After listening to Lenny play, Gebhard referred him to Helen Coates, a young woman from Rockford, Illinois, who had come to Boston to study with him and became his assistant. Each lesson with her cost six dollars. Because Sam was not being supportive of his son's ambition at the time, Lenny was under pressure to pay for the lessons himself. He did so by taking on various piano-playing jobs that came along.

Lenny's growing fascination with music had been of concern to Sam right from its start. It made him recollect an Old-World figure called a *klezmer*. A *klezmer* was a wandering musician. For a few kopecs and perhaps a little food, he would play music, usually on a violin, at weddings and bar mitzvahs. Jennie also had memories of the *klezmer*, and to her he was an enchanting figure. But to Sam a *klezmer* was lowly. The prospect of his son becoming some New-World version of a *klezmer* — perhaps a piano player in a cocktail lounge — distressed him.

Sam's hope was that Lenny would join him someday in the Samuel Bernstein Hair Company. In that way Sam would gain *nachas*, which means pleasure reflected through the achievement of someone else, often one's child. Becoming a rabbi was probably an alternative Sam would have found acceptable for Lenny, but certainly it was the only one.

Despite Sam's reservations, he did give Lenny's interest in music some support during its early years and even gained some *nachas* in return. It was Sam who had brought fourteen-year-old Lenny to his first concert, a performance by the Boston Pops, and they had both been swept away by Ravel's *Boléro*. Sam soon took Lenny to another concert, this time to hear the famous Sergei Rachmaninoff. When Lenny was older, Sam sometimes brought him along on cruises on which he would often be asked to entertain fellow passengers with his piano playing. And for a while, when Sam owned Avol Labortories, a new (and brief) business venture of his, the company sponsored a once-a-week, fifteen-minute radio program. It usually consisted of music performed by a pianist named Leonard Bernstein.

Even though Sam was occasionally supportive, his basic attitude while Lenny was growing up was that music was fine as a pastime but that, as he put it to his son, "if you're going to be a *mensch* and support a family, you can't be a *klezmer.*"

The message from Helen Coates was quite different. She quickly recognized not only Lenny's ability but also his affinity for music. She was a demanding teacher and also a kindly one. Before long she was scheduling Lenny's lessons for the end of the day, and although they were formally supposed to last an hour, they began to run longer.

Sharon was where Lenny enjoyed many summers, and it was the scene of some of his early creative musical adventures. In 1933, he staged a Jewish-inspired, lightheartedly modified version of Bizet's opera *Carmen* in the dining room of the local lakeside hotel. The girls and boys reversed roles, and Lenny himself played Carmen. The members of the supposedly all-male chorus were actually girls costumed as little old men; they even wore yarmulkes.

In later summers in Sharon, Lenny organized the production of two Gilbert and Sullivan operettas, first *The Mikado* and then *H.M.S. Pinafore*. In both he remained more faithful to the original version than he had with *Carmen*. However, he could not resist importing ballet music from Verdi's opera *Aida* into *Pinafore*. At a suitable moment the cue was given: "Bring on the Egyptian dancing girls." Shirley and the Kaplan twins entered, danced to the music from *Aida*, and exited. Gilbert and Sullivan's version of the operetta then continued.

*Lenny and friends performing, Singer's Inn, Sharon, summer of 1933*

In those years when Lenny was first developing his skills as a pianist, he was also going through school in the usual way. At eleven he had entered Class VI —the seventh grade — of the highly regarded Boston Latin School, and he continued his studies there for six years.

Boston Latin is the oldest school in America. It is even older than any American college, having opened in 1635, the year before Harvard was founded. Over the years, many illustrious Americans have attended it, including John Hancock, Samuel Adams, and Benjamin Franklin. The school celebrated its tercentenary — its three hundredth anniversary — during 1934-35, which happened to be Lenny's senior year.

During his years there, Lenny's overall musical ability came to be known and admired. As a senior, he was elected president of the Glee Club. Moreover, he wrote the music and, along with Lawrence F. Ebb, a very bright classmate, the words for their class song. At the end of their senior year, Lenny and Edward Merrill Goldman, another talented pianist, shared that year's award for excellence in music.

There had been one other interesting development between the start of Lenny's love for music at the age of ten and the end of his senior year in high school: he was feeling a good deal stronger, livelier, more robust. The music seemed somehow to be healing and invigorating him. It was also bringing him a sense of inner joy that would last throughout his lifetime.

In June 1935, he graduated from Boston Latin School. In September, seventy-eight of the school's graduates became freshmen in Harvard College, Leonard Bernstein, one among them.

# Undergraduate at Harvard

ost graduates of Boston Latin School who attended Harvard continued to live at home and commuted to college. Lenny, by contrast, was a residential student. As a freshman, he lived in Wigglesworth Hall, a long, narrow brick dormitory extending along much of one side of Harvard Yard. As an upperclassman, he lived in Eliot House, a stately residence outside the Yard, down by the Charles River.

Lenny chose music as his field of concentration. At Harvard, "studying music" took on a new meaning for him. Previously, it had meant, primarily, learning to play the piano. Here it meant, primarily, investigating the theory of music and analyzing the structure of musical compositions. Years later he told an audience that "you could spend hours wandering through the Music Building and never hear a note of actual music." As a senior he prepared an honors thesis exploring how American music reflects the ethnic backgrounds of its composers.

While at Harvard, Lenny continued to take piano lessons. At eighteen he was judged ready to study with Heinrich Gebhard. Under Gebhard's guidance, he crossed the boundary from accomplished amateur to fledgling professional. The two developed a warm relationship. When Gebhard's book, *The Art of Pedaling*, appeared many years later, it was his former student Leonard Bernstein who was invited to write its introduction.

Lenny's extracurricular life in college revolved around music. As a sophomore, he had already become program chairman of the Harvard Musical Club. Another of his interests was the Harvard Film Society, which presented silent movies, enriching the shows with live music on a piano. When Lenny was playing, he could make the audience all but forget about the movie.

He also tried his hand as a music critic. His articles demonstrated broad knowledge of music and talent as a writer. Mixed in with both was a youthful daring, bravado, and irreverence. One of his articles in *The Harvard Advocate*, the undergraduate literary magazine, begins:

> The first concert of the Boston Symphony Orchestra is over and eligible for review. By and large it was the traditional B.S.O. offering: magnificent precision, the unbreakable tradition of false notes in the French horn department, the phenomenon (in the Vivaldi) of seeing woodwinds blown and not hearing them, the remarkable industry of the percussion boys. . . .

While good-naturedly dishing it out in this way, he was, of course, cheerfully unaware of how soon the critics' spotlights would be falling on him with their almost inevitable mixture of gratification and sting.

During 1937, he met two musicians who would be important to him, personally and professionally, for a long time. One was Dimitri Mitropoulos, a famous conductor originally from Greece. Lenny met him when he was in the Boston area as guest conductor with the BSO. The other was Aaron Copland, a distinguished American composer. Lenny was introduced to him on a visit to New York. Both men heard Lenny play the piano almost as soon as they had met him, and both were impressed. It did not take Mitropoulos long to begin referring to him as "genius boy."

*Sever Hall in Harvard Yard*

## MUSIC
### The Cradle Will Rock
*Amateurs of Harvard Student Union in First Showing Here of Exciting Dram*

BY MORES SMITH

It takes a little time for some things to *re* culture. But secure in our intellectual *a* can endorse the latest fad or at almost every one else has forgot! not to pursue the second cour lished others the pioneering regard. It's a nice, comf bluff not only yoursel

"The Cradle *' an American le associate* *tion*

*The Playgoer*

"The Cradle Will Rock"
*At Sanders Theatre*

From the minute Shirley Mann began to sing "I'm Checking Home Now" till the ensemble's final triumphant warning that "The Cradle Will Rock," Marc Blitzstein's music drama had a sympathetic Sanders Theatre audience Saturday If the test of a good play is its grip on , then "The Cradle" was a sucess.

tudent Union production had more welcome reception. It had brilli- lyrics, enough humor, and ex- st—the whole com- e of steel un- stac

### THE HARVARD CRIMSON

## Student Union Thespians Will Give Timely Musical Drama

"*The Cradle Will Rock*" *Will Be Presented in Sanders Theatre Tomorrow*

For the first time in its history producing a play on its own power, the Student Union tomorrow night will present Marc Blitzstein's musical drama "The Cradle Will Rock" in Sanders Theatre at 8:30 o'clock.

The play which stirred New York or over a year has been de- Ns Alliance of the New lc drama of dern and and

There Blitzstein himself played the score on a piano, on a bare stage lighted only by a single spotlight. Although it was originally planned that the author-composer should merely play and describe the action, the actors rose spontaneously from their seats to deliver their lines for a performance which Archibald MacLeish, curator of the Nieman Collection of Journalism, has called "the most exciting evening of theatre this New York generation has ever seen."

MacLeish a Sponsor
Besides MacLeish the facu'

1938 A
1937 F
1936 F
1937 F
1937 F

HA
1230-38 *

## Proletarian Play Lays It On Thick and Plentifully

BY ELLIOT NORTON

Marc Blitzstein's music drama, "The Cradle Will Rock," which was hanned from Federal Theatre pro- n in New York, has

*Senior in Harvard College.* The Cradle Will Rock *received considerable newspaper coverage.*

Towards the end of his years in college, Lenny generated two musical flourishes. The first was a production of Aristophanes' *The Birds* for which he wrote the music and conducted the orchestra. It was done entirely in Greek, and *The New York Times* carried an article about it, uncommon attention for a collegiate play.

His other major musical achievement in that spring of 1939 came in a production of Marc Blitzstein's *The Cradle Will Rock*. Lenny was a prominent performer as well as the show's co-director.

*The Cradle Will Rock* is a serious musical play holding a special role in the history of the American theater. It is a Depression-era story about the conflict over establishing a union in Steeltown, U.S.A. In the latter part of the 1930s, it was especially controversial. Amidst great conflict and with some major eleventh-hour changes, it had opened in New York's Venice Theater on June 16, 1937. Author-composer Blitzstein himself had to appear, and he did so alone on the stage while members of the cast, scattered throughout the audience, performed right from their seats.

The Harvard Student Union's version of *Cradle* opened on the campus, in Sanders Theater, on May 27, 1939. Fifteen minutes before it was supposed to start, the theater was virtually empty. But then the crowd began arriving, and by the time the performance did start, the theater was full. Among those present was Marc Blitzstein.

The production, with its simple style, had a great deal in common with the version that had opened in New York nearly two years earlier, except that this time the actors were all on stage. Blitzstein enjoyed the show enormously and remarked that Lenny's playing of the score had been better than his own. After the show, they spent some time together. They shared a deep interest in the political issues at the foundation of the play, and as time passed, they became good friends.

The show got such an enthusiastic reception that a second performance was hastily scheduled for June 2. Several of Boston's leading critics saw one performance or the other, and their views were generally quite favorable.

There was one interesting bit of casting that may well have slipped by many in the audience. According to the program, one of the parts was being played by Shirley Mann. However, an article about the play appearing in *The Harvard Crimson,* the undergraduate newspaper, had revealed her real name. It was Shirley Bernstein. She was then just fifteen years old. Her big brother had bootlegged her into a college production.

On June 22, Lenny was one of 866 members of Harvard's class of 1939 to graduate. He received his A.B. degree *cum laude in musica.*

Not long before Commencement, an article in the *Crimson* had reported seniors' plans for their careers. The headline proclaimed: "Seniors Choose Business, Law, Medicine as Favored Vocations." Near the end, the article also mentioned that two members of the class were planning careers in music. One wanted to be a concert singer. The other was planning to be a composer.

*Mitropoulos greets Bernstein under the clock in the lobby of the Biltmore Hotel.*

# But Now What?

hortly after graduation, Bernstein headed for New York. There he moved in with Adolph Green, a New Yorker and a friend of his from a previous summer when they had worked together on a show at a children's camp. Green was a member of a group called the Revuers, which sang at a nightclub in Greenwich Village. During that summer Bernstein occasionally played as the group's accompanist. He also got a good taste of New York's musical and theatrical life, which was greatly to his liking. But as the summer drew to a close, the money was dwindling, and having no clear prospect of earning more, he travelled home, somewhat discouraged.

He had just returned when he learned that Dimitri Mitropoulos would be passing through New York. Bernstein hurried back to meet him face-to-face and seek his advice on what to do next. Mitropoulos told him that he had the makings of a fine conductor but needed further training. Bernstein approached the Julliard School of Music in New York only to find its enrollment already closed. Mitropoulos then arranged an audition for him with Fritz Reiner, head of the Conducting Department at the Curtis Institute of Music in Philadelphia.

When Bernstein arrived, Reiner wasted no time on small talk. A score lay open on the piano, its title not visible. It was a full orchestral score, which is much more complicated than a score for piano alone. Reiner asked him to identify it. Bernstein studied it closely. Somewhere in the music for the woodwinds he recognized the tune of a little ditty he had learned long ago, and it became his telltale clue. "Brahms! *The Academic Festival Overture.*"

"Good," said Reiner. "Now play it to the end."

His acceptance into Curtis was Bernstein's first piece of good fortune there. That his tuition was paid through the generosity of a total stranger was a second. Her name was Mary Louise Curtis Bok, and her wealth had come from the family's success in publishing. As the Curtis Institute's founder, she had endowed it so substantially that no student had to pay any tuition whatsoever. And to make things even better, the Institute loaned each student of piano, conducting, or composition, a grand piano for his or her entire stay.

Although Bernstein felt that Curtis' professional training was too intense, he did receive an outstanding education there. Isabelle Vengerova instructed him in piano. Where Gebhart had been courtly, she could be severe. Privately he referred to her as "tirana" — his way of calling her a tyrant — but she got him to listen carefully to his own playing, not just to go through a familiar piece mechanically. Reiner worked with him in conducting and, like Vengerova, was extremely demanding and precise; however, he eventually called Bernstein "the most talented all-around student I ever had." Randall Thompson, a composer as well as the conservatory's new director, taught him orchestration. Here things were less severe. Thompson and Bernstein shared a passion for crossword puzzles in the newspapers, and they would invariably work one before turning to the assignment.

*Teatime at Curtis. Bernstein and (clockwise), Fritz Reiner, Mary Louise Curtis Bok, Isabelle Vengerova, and Randall Thompson*

One day during his first year at Curtis, a newspaper article caught Bernstein's eye. It was about the opening that summer of a music school, the Berkshire Music Center. The Boston Symphony Orchestra was starting it as an expansion of its summer activities at Tanglewood, an estate in Lenox, Massachusetts. For Serge Koussevitzky, the BSO's conductor, the school was the fulfillment of a dream.

Along with many others, Bernstein applied. Sometime during April, he called on Koussevitzky, at Symphony Hall, the BSO's home in Boston. As an undergraduate, seated high up in the second balcony, he had watched Koussevitzky conduct many times, but now he was meeting him for the first time. Somewhere in the midst of their conversation, in his English with its strong reminder that he had spoken Russian first, Koussevitzky said: "Of course, my dear, I vill accept you in my class."

The Berkshire Music Center opened on July 8, 1940, with 312 students. President Roosevelt sent along his expression of good wishes. In an advanced group of only five students, Bernstein studied conducting with Koussevitzky, and they developed a warm, close relationship. He had no children, and Bernstein became like a son to him. With affection, Koussevitzky later came to call him "Lenyushka."

Whereas Reiner was logical and precise, Koussevitzky was intuitive and emotional. He once tried to let the musicians know when to start playing: "Ven my stick touches de air, you play."

"Now that says nothing," Bernstein later commented, "and yet it says everything. When you want an ethereal sound, as at the beginning of the Prelude to *Lohengrin,* a downbeat would be almost too crude. The 'stick touching the air' is really the effect you want."

Bernstein also recalled how Koussevitzky would try to get the orchestra to improve its playing of some piece of music: "Koussy used to say, 'Eet mus be more beautiful.' Nobody would know what was wrong or why it wasn't beautiful enough already. But they would try again and eventually it *was* more beautiful."

During the first summer at Tanglewood, Bernstein was having the time of his life. In a letter to his family, he communicated his boundless enthusiasm:

> . . .I have never seen such a beautiful setup in my life. I've been conducting the orchestra every
> morning, & I'm playing my first concert tomorrow night. Kouss gave me the hardest & longest
> number of all. . . . He is the most marvelous man — a beautiful spirit that never lags or fails. . .
> (I actually rode in his car with him today!). . . . We've been working very hard. . .the inspiration
> of this center is terrific enough to keep you going with no sleep at all. I'm so excited about
> tomorrow night — I wish you could all be here. . . .

At summer's end Bernstein returned to Curtis for his second and final year. The summer of 1941 found him back at Tanglewood, again studying under Koussevitzky, having a wonderful time, and exhibiting a flair for what he was doing. That flair was not lost on Howard Taubman of *The New York Times*, whose column on August 2 noted: "The young conductor who has made the biggest splash among Mr. Koussevitzky's group of handpicked students is Leonard Bernstein. . . ."

That winter he remained in Boston, but things did not go especially well. A BSO concert in which he was to be the piano soloist was cancelled. He opened a studio to teach piano but was not successful in obtaining students. In December, America became actively embroiled in World War II. Because of his asthma, Bernstein had already been turned down for military service; he very much regretted this situation but was unable to alter it.

He returned to Tanglewood for the summer of 1942, no longer as a student but as Koussevitzky's assistant. The BSO's summer concerts there had been discontinued for the duration of the war, but the Berkshire Music Center carried on for that one additional summer before its activities were also suspended.

In the fall of 1942, he decided to try his luck once more in New York. Again, things were not easy. He did perform for the troops at Fort Dix, New Jersey, as a way of contributing to the war effort, but work for pay was hard to come by. Finally, after several months, he landed a job, paying twenty-five dollars a week, at the music publishing firm of Harms-Remick. His main assignment was to listen to jazz recordings that the performers had simply improvised and then, using conventional staff notation, to write down the music so that it could be published.

Even though this work actually required great musical skill, Bernstein worried that it might somehow devalue his good name as a talented and serious musician. As a result, he did it using the pseudonym Lenny Amber. This name was not chosen at random, however, because "Bernstein" can be translated from German as "amber stone."

*Koussevitzky and Bernstein, after a performance, 1949*

Earlier and for quite a different reason, Koussevitzky had suggested that Bernstein truly change his name. The new name he proposed was Leonard S. Burns. (The S. was for "Samuelovich," to honor his father.) Koussevitzky, who had himself converted away from Judaism, thought that Bernstein would improve his chance to have a successful career in the world of music if he were to conceal his Jewish heritage. Despite Bernstein's respect for his mentor, it did not take him very long to make up his mind, and when he did, his conviction was absolute. He would "make it with the name Leonard Bernstein or not at all."

Bernstein's musical interests were so broad that conducting and performing as a pianist were not enough; he wanted to compose as well. Towards the end of 1942, his attention was focused on a competition sponsored by the New England Conservatory of Music.

December 31 was the deadline, and as it neared, he was working feverishly to complete his first symphony, the *Jeremiah Symphony*. Shirley and some friends were helping, handling the mechanical part of preparing the score, while his current girlfriend made sure the supply of coffee was ample. When the score was at last ready, there was no time to send it by mail, and so Bernstein rushed to Boston, managing — just barely — to submit it on time.

When the results were later announced, he was disappointed because his symphony did not win. Even worse, Koussevitzky indicated that he did not much care for the work. Eventually, however, it began to get some important recognition. Reiner, who was also the Pittsburgh Symphony's conductor, invited him to perform it with that orchestra in January 1944, and even Koussevitzky arranged for him to present it with the BSO soon thereafter. Several months later, it won the New York Music Critics Circle Award as the "most outstanding orchestral work by an American composer introduced during the 1943-44 season."

Although Tanglewood's regular summer activities were not taking place in 1943, Koussevitzky was staying at his home nearby. He invited Bernstein to participate with him in some musical activity for the benefit of the Red Cross.

The chance to leave New York in August for a visit in the Berkshires was welcome, and Shirley and Helen Coates joined him on the trip. After arriving, Bernstein learned that Artur Rodzinski, another summer resident of the area, Koussevitzky's friend, and the newly appointed Musical Director of the Philharmonic-Symphony Society of New York — less formally called the New York Philharmonic — wanted to see him. The next morning he went to call on Rodzinski at his goat farm. They talked outdoors, sitting on a haystack. When Bernstein returned to Shirley and Helen Coates, he announced simply: "Meet the new assistant conductor of the New York Philharmonic." The date was August 25, 1943. It was his twenty-fifth birthday.

A few days later, he saw a newspaper's announcement of his appointment. He sent the clipping along to Helen Coates. On it he had written: "Here we go! Love, Lenny."

Soon he took up his new post as assistant conductor, but the two components of the title were not at all evenly balanced. With all kinds of details assigned to him, he was doing a great deal of assisting and very little conducting. To his family he confided his expectation that they would have to wait a long time to see him conduct the New York Philharmonic.

*Carnegie Hall, as it looked in 1943*

# Ready When the Call Came

s the weekend of November 13 and 14, 1943 approached, Bernstein was expecting Jennie Tourel's song recital at Town Hall on Saturday evening to be its highlight. His cycle of five "kid songs" entitled *I Hate Music* was on her program. It was the best thing that had yet happened to him as a composer, and his parents were travelling to New York by train for the occasion and bringing eleven-year-old Burtie along too.

Rodzinski was away for a brief holiday at his farm, and the distinguished Bruno Walter was appearing with the Philharmonic as its guest conductor. After Friday's concert, Walter informed Bruno Zirato, the Philharmonic's assistant manager, that he was not feeling well. By Saturday he was much worse. Zirato told Bernstein to stand by.

Even so, when Bernstein set out for the recital, he thought the prospect of actually being called upon to conduct the Philharmonic the following afternoon was remote. Jennie Tourel's recital went extremely well, and Bernstein's presence was warmly acknowledged. A lively party at her apartment capped off the evening, and by the time he arrived home and made his way into bed, it was around 4 A.M.

By 9 A.M. Bernstein had the news. Walter was too ill to appear that afternoon, and he would indeed conduct. Because the Sunday afternoon concerts were broadcast over the CBS radio network, there would be a vast number of listeners in addition to those present in Carnegie Hall.

Bernstein called his parents at their hotel and told them that three tickets for the conductor's box would be waiting for them at Carnegie Hall. He telephoned Shirley, then a student at Mount Holyoke College, and told her to listen. He also let Koussevitzky know. When he went to see Bruno Walter, he found him wrapped in blankets and shivering. After they reviewed the program, Bernstein returned to his small apartment. When it was time to dress, he put on a double-breasted gray suit, the best substitute he owned for the more formal attire a conductor would typically wear for an afternoon concert.

It is always difficult to announce, at the last minute, the replacement of a celebrated conductor by a virtual unknown. When Zirato informed the audience of the substitution, Bernstein, waiting in the wings, heard some groans. Zirato tried to strike a positive note: "We are now going to witness the debut of a full-fledged American conductor, born and entirely trained in this country."

The concert began with the Overture to *Manfred* by Robert Schumann. Its opening three chords are tricky. When they came out pure and strong and sharp, they became the prologue for an excellent concert to follow. In later years, Bernstein was fond of saying that those opening chords were his only distinct, direct memory of the concert itself. Burton's recollection of his brother's triumph, nearly forty years after the event, was more vivid. The ovation at the concert's conclusion was "the loudest human sound I had ever heard."

On Monday, the concert was front-page news in *The New York Times* and the *New York Herald Tribune.* Leonard Bernstein had suddenly become famous.

On the Town. *Its original run of 463 performances was a long one in the 1940s.*

# Dreams Coming True

ernstein's debut in Carnegie Hall gave his career a spectacular boost. Almost immediately he began a whirlwind of activity. During 1944, he travelled some fifty thousand miles to make about ninety guest-conducting appearances. His popularity rapidly raised his stature above that of an assistant conductor, and the Philharmonic responded by making him a full-fledged guest conductor for the 1944-45 season.

Busy as he was conducting, Bernstein had the enthusiasm and, somehow, also the energy to compose. Early in 1944, a young dancer and choreographer named Jerome Robbins was preparing a new ballet and asked him to write its music. *Fancy Free*, about three sailors on furlough in New York and eager to meet girls, premiered on April 18, 1944, at New York's Metropolitan Opera House with Bernstein conducting. One observer recalled:

> At its conclusion there was a genuine ovation with approximately twenty curtains and a house cheering from its heart. The seven dancers and Bernstein stood hand in hand almost like children, afraid to believe their senses, delighted, timid and dazed.

*Fancy Free*'s success prompted Bernstein, Robbins, Adolph Green, and Betty Comden — Green's partner — to develop it into a musical comedy. Some of the early work took place in an unusual setting: a hospital. When, by coincidence, Bernstein and Green both happened to need surgery, they scheduled their operations so that they would be in the hospital together and able to work on the show while recuperating. Their joint convalescence was something of a show in itself, accompanied by music, singing, gin rummy, and the general atmosphere of a lively show-business cocktail party. They also made some progress on the real show.

*On the Town* opened at New York's Adelphi Theater on December 28, 1944. Like *Fancy Free*, it was set in New York, and "New York, New York" became its most enduring song. *On the Town* was received with such great enthusiasm that it ran for 463 performances.

Before arriving in New York, *On the Town* had opened for a pre-Broadway trial in Boston. Even though the show was well received there, the occasion caused Bernstein substantial anguish as well as pleasure because Koussevitzky criticized him severely over his interest in popular music and its interference with his concentration on classical music. As time passed, others would also challenge the breadth of his musical interests, but to have the issue raised so forcefully by Koussevitzky, of all people, was especially unpleasant.

In the fall of 1945, Bernstein did assume an important position of the sort Koussevitzky had in mind: conductor of the New York City Symphony. The orchestra's home was in the New York City Center of Music and Drama on West Fifty-fifth Street. Here Bernstein developed a loyal following among music lovers with a taste for programs somewhat more innovative and modern than those the Philharmonic usually presented. But although the endeavor was an artistic success, it was not workable financially and, after three seasons, when finances were promising to get worse, Bernstein resigned. Shortly after his resignation, the orchestra itself folded.

*Despite the dangers of war, music in Beersheba, November 20, 1948*

Early in his career, Bernstein began appearing outside the United States, initially in Canada and then overseas. He first conducted in Europe in May 1946, at a festival in Prague celebrating the Czech Symphony Orchestra's fiftieth anniversary. In June he went abroad again. His popularity was growing beyond America's borders. His horizons had become truly international.

With Israel, Bernstein enjoyed a special relationship, and the affection was both deep and mutual. He had first travelled to the area in April 1947, thirteen months before Israel had even become an independent nation. On that tour he led the Palestine Philharmonic Orchestra — soon to become the Israel Philharmonic Orchestra — in nine concerts. Writing about the first, Peter Gradenwitz reported in *The New York Times:*

The enthusiasm of the audience...knew no bounds, and not since the days of Arturo Toscanini — who, as you will remember, launched our orchestra on its way ten years ago — has a conductor been recalled so many times and been given a similar ovation.

Afterwards, when Bernstein wanted to express that some occasion had been an outstandingly spectacular success, he would often just say: "It was like Israel."

During the fall of 1948, Bernstein returned for an extended visit. Now an independent nation, Israel was engulfed in war. The war had begun in May when the surrounding Arab nations, intent upon destroying Israel, had attacked it within eight hours of its birth.

The pace of his schedule was challenging. He conducted forty concerts and also performed as piano soloist in thirty-two of them. Reminders and threats of war were never far away. On one occasion, he accompanied a small group of musicians on a dangerous trip by bus to Beersheba to give a concert right after the town's liberation. At another concert, he led the orchestra without any interruption, despite the menacing howl of two air raid alarms. Afterwards, Bernstein remarked: "I never played such an adagio. I thought it was my swan song." On still another occasion, as several thousand soldiers and civilians looked on and cheered, Bernstein was given the Defense of Jerusalem Medal. It honored him for "unusual and hazardous service performed for the Israeli nation during time of war in travelling along dangerous roads to conduct...in embattled Jerusalem." To the young nation, he was a hero of major proportions.

When the Israel Philharmonic Orchestra made its first tour of the United States and Canada, early in 1951, Bernstein and Koussevitsky shared the conducting. The orchestra visited forty cities and gave fifty-five concerts in ten weeks.

Late in the spring of 1951, Bernstein was eager to withdraw from guest-conducting for a short sabbatical devoted to composing. In 1949 he had completed his second symphony, *The Age of Anxiety*, a work inspired by W. H. Auden's poem of the same name. The piece was awarded the Hornblit Prize as the best new work performed by the Boston Symphony Orchestra for that season. But composing in brief, hurried snatches while travelling had been difficult. Moreover, he had not found time to compose much else in recent years. A sabbatical was in order. Bernstein rented a place in Cuernavaca, a lovely spot in Mexico, and at the beginning of June, he arrived and settled in.

That sabbatical was not to be. Right after his arrival, word came that Koussevitzky was gravely ill. Bernstein rushed to Boston. On the evening of June 3, Bernstein visited him in the hospital. The next day, with his wife Olga and his "Lenyushka" there, Koussevitzky died.

For Bernstein, it was a great loss. In the eleven years they had known one another, Koussevitzky had been his mentor. But Bernstein could take comfort in knowing that the relationship had not been at all one-sided. One important gift the apprentice had given the master was to rekindle somewhat his pride in his own Jewish heritage.

At Tanglewood's opening that year, Bernstein spoke movingly about him. And then he went to work. There were students to train and concerts to conduct. The work that had been so dear to Koussevitzky had to go on. Cuernavaca was far away.

In addition to sorrow, 1951 also brought Bernstein new happiness; on September 9, he and Felicia Montealegre Cohn were married. They had first met in 1946 — on February 6, her birthday, as a matter of fact — and before the year was out, they had become engaged. But as a talented and refined young actress, she was also in the early stages of building a career, and under the weight of two budding careers, the engagement was broken. In 1951, however, their romance flowered anew. According to Burton, "It was finally apparent to both of them that if they were ever going to marry, it would be to each other."

*Marriage: September 9, 1951. His suit had been Koussevitzky's.*

Their marriage took place in Boston, at Temple Mishkan Tefila. Felicia had converted to Judaism. Having a Jewish father made her half-Jewish, but her mother was a Latin American aristocrat. Felicia, who had been born in Costa Rica and grown up in Chile, had been raised as a Catholic. It was not exactly what Sam and Jennie had had in mind for their son, but in grandchildren there would be much *nachas*, and that prospect subdued their apprehensions.

Few, if any, music-related activities appealed to Bernstein more than teaching, and in 1951-52 he joined the faculty of Brandeis University in Waltham, Massachusetts. Learning and intellectual pursuits were high on his list of priorities, and Bernstein respected his students' creative potential. Like Israel, Brandeis was then a very new enterprise, and Bernstein helped found its School of Creative Arts and taught there for two years, travelling from New York, at first weekly and then monthly, to do so.

He is well remembered in Brandeis' early history for having staged its first Festival of the Creative Arts in 1952 and the second, in 1953. Among the attractions of the first was the premiere of *Trouble in Tahiti*, his brief opera in which he continued to explore themes introduced in *The Age of Anxiety*: loneliness, isolation, and despair in the modern world.

*With Isaac Stern in Venice, chatting by a canal*

During Bernstein's second year at Brandeis, Broadway beckoned again. The successful play *My Sister Eileen* was being turned into a musical. Earlier he and his pals Comden and Green had declined an invitation to write its words and music, and the producers had turned to others instead. However, when the scheduled opening was only six weeks away, the producers suddenly realized that the music was not coming together, that it was, in fact, a disaster. They went back to Bernstein, Comden, and Green and again asked them to take on the assignment. This time, sensitive to the desperate situation and attracted by the challenge, they accepted.

With a minimum of two weeks needed for rehearsal, they had just four weeks in which to write the words and music for this show about two sisters from Ohio who move to New York. They worked in the "thinking room" in Bernstein's apartment, amidst clouds of cigarette smoke. Somehow, they finished in time, and not just passably but spectacularly well. *Wonderful Town* opened on Broadway on February 25, 1953. It won the New York Drama Critics' award as the year's best musical and ran for 553 performances.

During the first half of the 1950s, Bernstein experienced some major successes in Italy. In 1950, he conducted a concert at Milan's Teatro alla Scala. For an American to have been asked to conduct there at all was an honor. Still, it is as an opera house, not a concert hall, that La Scala is truly legendary. To lead an opera there would be an even higher honor. Three years later, Bernstein was invited back to conduct one.

A performance of Cherubini's *Medea*, starring the tempestuous soprano Maria Callas and conducted by Victor de Sabata, had been scheduled for December 10, 1953. As the date approached, Sabata had to cancel. Others were available to step in, but Bernstein happened to be in Italy, and it was Bernstein whom Callas wanted. At first he was hesitant, but when she appealed to him personally over the telephone, he accepted.

Fritz Reiner once summed up why it is considerably more challenging to put on an opera than a concert by observing that "so much more can go wrong." But on this occasion, little, if anything, did go wrong, and one critic pronounced the result "indisputably brilliant." Bernstein had become the first American to conduct at La Scala during its regular opera season.

Less than a year later, early in the autumn of 1954, Venice was the scene of another triumph, the premiere of *Serenade*, his orchestral work for solo violin, string orchestra, and percussion. Again, a literary work had provided a spark of creativity; in this case, it was Plato's *Symposium.* For the premiere, Bernstein conducted while his friend and colleague Isaac Stern played the violin solo. At thirty-four, Stern, whose debut at Carnegie Hall had also been in 1943, was already regarded as one of the world's virtuoso violinists. For his part in the premiere of *Serenade*, Stern was described in *The New York Times* as an "incomparable soloist."

West Side Story *on Broadway. Juliet had a balcony. Maria has a fire escape.*

In December 1956, another show with music by Leonard Bernstein opened on Broadway. *Candide* was based upon Voltaire's satire about a young man inclined to believe that this was the best of all possible worlds because his teacher had told him so, while one bleak experience of his after another was making the notion seem ridiculous. Bernstein's music received glowing reviews, but those for the show itself were mixed. Walter Kerr of the *Herald Tribune* called it "a really spectacular disaster." After only seventy-three performances it closed.

There was good reason why any letdown Bernstein might have felt over *Candide*'s fate could be minimal and brief. Even before its opening, he had been at work on another musical for Broadway and one destined to have a very different reception.

*West Side Story* has become part of the cultural landscape, and its music is one of Bernstein's major achievements. It had an initial run on Broadway of 734 performances, then went on tour for ten months before returning to Broadway for 249 additional performances. The movie version, released in 1961, won ten Oscars, including the one for best picture.

Reminiscing late in his life, Bernstein recalled that it had all started in 1949 when Jerome Robbins first approached him and Arthur Laurents, who ultimately wrote the book, about creating a modern American version of Shakespeare's *Romeo and Juliet*. Originally the underlying feud was to be between Catholics and Jews, and the show was to be set on New York's East Side during the Easter-Passover season and called *East Side Story*. But the project never developed very far in that form.

Some years later, Bernstein was in California in connection with his score for the movie *On the Waterfront*. One day when he and Laurents were relaxing around the pool at the Beverly Hills Hotel and again thinking about the show, some newspaper headlines that caught their attention sparked the idea for the feud to be between two rival gangs with different ethnic backgrounds. That concept took hold, and the setting became New York's Upper West Side.

Bernstein remembered the creation of *West Side Story* as "one of the most extraordinary collaborations of my life, perhaps *the* most, in that very sense of our nourishing one another." In addition to Robbins, Laurents, and Bernstein, there was a fourth major creative figure, a young man who had never before written lyrics for a Broadway show but who Bernstein sensed was a great new talent. His name was Stephen Sondheim.

The final preparations for Broadway included brief trials in Washington and Philadelphia. Then, on September 26, 1957, some eight years after Robbins, Laurents, and Bernstein's initial conversation, *West Side Story* opened in New York's Winter Garden Theater.

Bernstein hardly had time to pause over the reviews. He was heading for Israel. The Fredric R. Mann Auditorium was being dedicated with a gala concert on October 2 in Tel Aviv, and some of the orchestra's most cherished friends had been invited to participate. Isaac Stern, pianist Artur Rubinstein, and cellist Paul Tortelier were the solosits. The conductor was Leonard Bernstein.

*Moscow. A visit by the New York Philharmonic, on tour under Bernstein, in 1959*

# A Position of Leadership

I n the mid-1950s, the New York Philharmonic was in the doldrums. Dimitri Mitropoulos had served as Musical Director since 1951-52. In the spring of 1956, both Howard Taubman of the *Times* and Paul Henry Lang, his scholarly counterpart on the *Herald Tribune,* believed the time had come for someone else to take over, and each wrote bluntly saying so. Their opinions were not the only factors, but they were certainly influential. Major changes were soon under way. By the beginning of the 1958-59 season, Leonard Bernstein had assumed sole musical leadership of the New York Philharmonic with the title, now slightly modified, of Music Director.

During his years with the Philharmonic, Bernstein often led it on tours abroad. He never formally held the title of American Ambassador, but informally he was exactly that.

An especially memorable tour took place during the late summer and early fall of 1959. It began in Athens, ended in London, and had twenty-seven other destinations in between. For Bernstein, its most significant portion was the three-week visit to Soviet Russia. For the first time, he was visiting the land of his ancestors, the land which both of his parents had left half a century earlier.

Felicia travelled with him. Shortly after arriving in Moscow, Bernstein called his father and put him on the telephone with his younger brother, Shlomo, whom he had not seen since 1908. Sam then decided to join them. Unfortunately, the long separation had left the brothers with little to say to one another, and the reunion was flat. As a son and nephew, Bernstein was disappointed at the anticlimax.

A high point of the trip for Bernstein was the opportunity to meet Boris Pasternak, a man well respected in the West as a Nobel Prize winner in literature but far out of favor with the Soviet authorities for his unflattering portrayal of life under Communism. The Bernsteins and Pasternaks spent an evening together. Pasternak also attended a concert, telling Bernstein after it: "Thank you for having taken us into Heaven. Now we must return to Earth."

More tours followed. Extensive travel was not new to the Philharmonic, but under Bernstein, tours took on an enhanced animation and liveliness.

The larger, more fundamental challenge was to rejuvenate the orchestra at home. It was not a single-handed effort. Behind the scenes, other members of the Philharmonic's family were also working very hard. But Bernstein was the central figure in the agenda for change.

He was eager to try new things. At the outset, he replaced the formal concert on Thursday evenings with an informal one known as a "Preview." A new format called for a new wardrobe. The one he selected for the orchestra was untraditional, to say the least. Upon seeing a colleague in the new attire, one musician could not resist telling him: "You look like a bellhop at the Astor." The uniforms did not make it through the first season.

The Preview concerts themselves fared much better, at least initially. Their format called for Bernstein to teach about the music as well as to conduct it, and if singing would help to

*A Young People's Concert reaching far beyond the concert hall*

make a point, he would sing. At first, the Previews were highly popular, and tickets were hard to come by. In time, however, the format lost its luster and was discontinued.

In 1962, the Philharmonic moved into a home of its own for the first time in its history: Philharmonic Hall in Lincoln Center. (About a decade later, its name was changed to Avery Fisher Hall.) On September 23, Bernstein conducted the inaugural concert amidst much ceremony and celebration. At the outset, the hall had many acoustical problems, and it was many years before it was generally accepted that they had been satisfactorily corrected.

One hallmark of Bernstein's years with the Philharmonic was that, like Koussevitsky before him, he championed American composers, and their work gained greater representation in the orchestra's programs than ever before. Distinguished American composers such as Aaron Copland, Samuel Barber, Lukas Foss, Roy Harris, Charles Ives, Walter Piston, William Schuman, and Randall Thompson gained an appropriate place in the repertory.

Despite all of his other responsibilities, Bernstein's enthusiasm to teach remained compelling and irrepressible. The Young People's Concerts provided an excellent forum for expressing it. The Philharmonic had been presenting them since 1924, but during Bernstein's tenure they gained a new stature and much wider audience through the advent of television and his skill in using it.

He appeared in fifty-three televised Young People's Concerts between 1958 and 1972. However, his initial experience teaching on television had preceded the first of them by more than three years. That milestone had occurred in 1954 — on November 14, coincidentally enough — on a program called *Omnibus*. With this and similar presentations, he had accumulated considerable experience teaching on television prior to his first Young People's Concert.

The audience for the Young People's Concerts had two quite different components: those present in the concert hall, numbering several thousand, and those watching on television, numbering in the millions. Although the programs were nominally for ''young people,'' many adults enjoyed and learned from them. Sometimes a puzzled parent would watch simply out of curiosity to learn what magic was transforming an otherwise rambunctious child into an attentive student of classical music.

Young and old, the public warmly embraced Bernstein. A human warmth also emerged between Bernstein and members of the orchestra. One musician communicated it quite simply: ''We worshipped Toscanini, but we love Lenny.''

With the New York music critics, it was a distinctly different story. They formed the one main constituency from which Bernstein did not get consistent raves. They admired his talent, but his flamboyant style often exasperated them, and a review would, at times, sound like a scolding from a stern, indignant, impatient parent.

The clash is easy to understand. Classical music critics tend to approach their topic in a highly studious, analytical way. Off-stage, Bernstein was every bit as intellectual. But once he ascended the podium, that aspect of his approach was not at all what people saw. Instead,

*Nina, Jamie, and Alexander (left to right) enjoy a playful moment with their parents. 1968.*

they saw an animated, high-spirited conductor for whom the music was totally captivating. So absorbed did he become that the baton would even, on a rare occasion, go flying out of his hand as he swung his arms and danced vibrantly around the podium, exhorting the musicians to make the music ever more beautiful and expressive. Many in the broader public adored his style, but it often left the critics tut-tutting.

Stung by their barbs, Bernstein on one occasion decided to conduct unemotionally. His reward was a musician asking him whether he had not been feeling well. That was the end of that. He went back to doing it his own way. In time, however, both Bernstein and the critics became more mellow.

In a world usually warm but occasionally chilly, it was nice for Bernstein to have a family. He and Felicia had three children. Jamie was a first anniversary present for her parents, delivered one day early: on September 8, 1952. Alexander Serge — named for Koussevitsky who had been Serge Alexander — was born on July 7, 1955; and Nina, on February 28, 1962.

When the children were young, Felicia helped guide and make their lives orderly on a day-to-day basis. One of the nice outcomes of their early years with parents gifted in language was that each became fluent in Spanish as well as English.

Their father liked playing with them, doing word games, and taking ski trips. He also liked to teach them. Jamie has recalled growing up with a ''mini-Young People's Concert'' regularly in progress at home. The teaching was not at all limited to music. When it was time for Alexander to begin preparing for his bar mitzvah, Bernstein took a lively interest not just in his overall progress but in its details. He sought guidance on his son's behalf from Goldie Feinsilver — formerly Miss Gans, his own teacher in Hebrew school some forty years earlier.

In the 1964-65 season, Bernstein took a sabbatical to compose. Thirteen months after resuming his duties, he surprised many people by announcing that he would be stepping down as Music Director. The change would not come until the end of the 1968-69 season, two and a half years later.

Bernstein's years with the Philharmonic were filled with high achievement, both for himself and for the orchestra. During that time, in addition to everything else, he had finished his own third symphony, called *Kaddish*, conducted the Metropolitan Opera for the first time, and completed three books.

As for the orchestra, it dramatically increased its audience, improved its finances, began a variety of new programs, and enhanced its educational offerings. Under Bernstein's leadership, the Philharmonic achieved a renaissance.

When he left as Music Director, in the spring of 1969, there was indeed a separation, but it was partial, not total. The orchestra's trustees had created, and bestowed upon him for life, a new position: Laureate Conductor. The orchestra gave him a mezuzah made of silver and gold.

Thirteen days after he conducted his last concert as Music Director, he suffered a separation that was permanent and painful: his father died.

*The Opera House in the John F. Kennedy Center for the Performing Arts, Washington, D.C.*

## Lofty Podium and Bully Pulpit

arly in his son's life, Sam had warned him about the financial hazards of a musical career. His concern had been quite appropriate to ordinary circumstances, and how could he have known how successful his son would become? Addressing this dilemma much later, Sam explained: "The Talmud teaches us, 'Don't expect miracles.'... You don't expect your child to be a Moses, a Maimonides, a Leonard Bernstein...."

Leonard Bernstein had indeed become an exception. His artistic success had brought financial reward and, with it, the need to manage his expanding affairs in an orderly way. In 1959, Amberson Enterprises, Inc. had been created to oversee many of his commercial endeavors. Shortly after he left the Philharmonic, an affiliated company, Amberson Productions, Inc., was formed. Schuyler Chapin, a man whom Bernstein had known for a decade and who was well versed in the managerial aspects of the world of music, became its executive producer.

The first project was to film a Bernstein-conducted performance of Verdi's *Requiem* in St. Paul's Cathedral in London. With all of the standard details to arrange, the new executive producer had his hands full. And, as he later wrote, he had one other problem too.

Bernstein was a heavy and incorrigible smoker. When Chapin arrived for the filming, the dean informed him that smoking was forbidden within the Cathedral. Chapin managed to help Bernstein get around the prohibition by locating a secluded lavatory, up a drafty, spiral staircase, outside his makeshift dressing room and office. There he could smoke undetected.

Later that evening, between the main performance and the retakes required for the filming, Bernstein said mournfully and within earshot of the dean: "I'd give anything for a cigarette, anything." The dean relented. "Mr. Bernstein, after what you've given us tonight, the unbelievable beauty of it that I shall never, never forget...please, smoke as much as you want!" Bernstein was soon smoking to his heart's delight.

The evening of September 8, 1971 was one of both high honor and high emotion for Bernstein. After years of preparation, the John F. Kennedy Center for the Performing Arts — Washington's only memorial to President Kennedy — was opening, bringing to an end the era when the nation's capital had no cultural center suitable to its stature. Bernstein had been commissioned to compose a work for the occasion.

It was altogether fitting that the commission had come to him. He and the President had shared many liberal ideals. In addition, he had performed at the celebration of Kennedy's inaugural as well as in the White House during his presidency. Bernstein had been thoroughly devastated by Kennedy's assassination and had subsequently dedicated his third symphony, *Kaddish*, "to the beloved memory of John F. Kennedy."

His composition for the opening of the Kennedy Center was *Mass*. Subtitled "a theater piece for singers, players, and dancers," it was his effort to adapt the Roman Catholic Mass to

*Thousands of people from all over the world flock to Tanglewood each summer.*

the setting of the theater. The critics' reactions were mixed. *Time* took the occasion to remind its readers that "Bernstein, after all, is an artist and entertainer, not a theologian."

When it was over, *Time* noted, "Bernstein wept helplessly as the audience thundered its applause, then launched into a marathon fit of kissing everyone in reach." And how would Kennedy have responded to *Mass*? "Jack would have loved it," according to Rose Kennedy, his eighty-one-year-old mother. "It's the great expression of hope that is important...."

Each summer at Tanglewood, the BSO operated both its music school, the Berkshire Music Center, and its program of concerts, the Berkshire Music Festival. (By the summer season of 1985, their formal names had become, respectively, the Tanglewood Music Center and the Tanglewood Music Festival.) When Gunther Schuller, Seiji Ozawa, and Bernstein came together in 1970 to form a troika to run Tanglewood, it was a sign of changes to come.

An important change was the amount of time Bernstein spent there. After his joyful summer in 1940, Tanglewood always remained close to his heart, but from 1952 through the

1960s, he performed and taught there on only a limited basis. In most of the next twenty-one years, things were different.

During this period, a typical visit would last ten days to two weeks. He would arrive with his colorful entourage and would soon be seen riding around the grounds, greeting admirers and signing autographs. Bernstein would conduct the BSO for the annual Serge and Olga Koussevitzky Memorial Concert.

He focused a great deal of attention on the Music Center's students. In the large living room at Saranak, which had been Koussevitzky's home, he would teach the young conductors, and he would share conducting the Music Center Orchestra with them. Late into an evening, he would join the students in partying. Some, while dancing, could be seen high off the ground, legs tucked up, in an acrobatic jump affectionately called "Lenny's leap" in honor of one of his more exuberant moves on the podium. Being around the students delighted him as much as it thrilled them.

Almost entirely across Massachusetts from Tanglewood lies Cambridge, home of Bernstein's alma mater. He had been invited to return there as the Charles Eliot Norton Professor of Poetry for the academic year 1972-73. The Norton Professor was to give a series of lectures and to make them available for publication.

Bernstein took up residence in Eliot House for a portion of the year. As usual, he plunged in with gusto. He visited classes, played squash (with Jamie, then an undergraduate, for one), went to students' parties, and made himself available for "endless rap sessions." As time passed, the preparation of the lectures was falling behind schedule, and so, in a tradition well understood by undergraduates, he arranged an extension and postponed them to the fall of 1973-74.

The lectures were intellectually ambitious. Calling them "The Unanswered Question," after one of Charles Ives' musical compositions, Bernstein explored the link between music and language — the grammar of music — as well as the tension within music between tonality and atonality. And here was no leaping, lunging, highly emotive conductor but, instead, someone sounding very much like a professor of music.

In seeking to cross intellectual boundaries, Bernstein did not limit himself to the one between music and linguistics. Like Theodore Roosevelt, who had described the presidency as a "bully pulpit" because it provided him such an excellent vantage point from which to speak and be heard, Leonard Bernstein also found that he had a bully pulpit. The high stature he had earned in music gave him opportunities to express himself, and be listened to, on topics other than music, and he accepted them gladly.

His interest in social issues was long-standing. His work on *The Cradle Will Rock* in college was one early manifestation of it. During the era of the Vietnam War, he was strongly opposed to America's participation, as was Felicia. They both worked with great dedication on behalf of Senator Eugene McCarthy's antiwar candidacy for the Democratic Party's presidential nomination in 1968. In mid-August, Bernstein spoke at a huge McCarthy rally in New York's Madison Square Garden. Over four years later, with the war still in progress, he conducted a concert in protest of it in the Washington National Cathedral, on the eve of President Nixon's second inaugural. The music was Haydn's *Mass in Time of War* with its poignant ending: "Dona Nobis Pacem" — "Give us peace."

Bernstein's interests extended to civil rights as well. Among all of the events in which he ever participated, the one simultaneously most celebrated and most controversial was a gathering he and Felicia hosted in January 1970 to help the Black Panthers — a political group deeply entangled in America's social turbulence — raise funds for the legal defense of members charged with crimes. Some journalists were invited, and the decision to include them backfired totally. The Bernsteins' efforts were promptly attacked in the *Times* and, not long afterwards, gleefully ridiculed in an article by Tom Wolfe in the magazine *New York*. Among other things, the article introduced the phrase "radical chic."

As intently as Bernstein cared about broad social issues, music was never far from his heart and mind. During the seventies and eighties, he continued composing, and he also continued conducting in many places throughout the world. One high moment was a concert at the Vatican in June 1973. Pope Paul VI attended, saying after it: "Here is an American who gives us old Europeans a music lesson." The *Times* made the comment its "Quotation of the Day."

Bernstein's reception was particularly warm in Vienna. Its distinguished musical lineage — including, among others, Haydn, Beethoven, Mozart, and Schubert — made that warmth especially pleasing. Speaking lightheartedly around the time he went there in 1968 to conduct Richard Strauss' *Der Rosenkavalier*, Bernstein commented: "Every taxi driver in Vienna knows the score better than I do." Nevertheless, the audience apparently thought he knew it rather well too because the performance he conducted earned a stunning ovation and forty-eight curtain calls. And when it came time to commemorate the bicentennial of Beethoven's birth in 1970, it was not one of the famous Europeans, but rather Bernstein, who was invited to Vienna to conduct *Fidelio*, the only opera Beethoven ever wrote. The admiration accorded him in Vienna tended to elevate the respect he received within American musical circles.

Bernstein's presentations of Beethoven's music, though greatly admired, did not improve Beethoven's reputation. How could they? But for another European composer, the situation was quite different. Over the years, Bernstein played a major role in enhancing the reputation of Gustav Mahler.

Bernstein and Mahler have been described as soulmates. They were both Jewish, deeply concerned with matters of faith, and very emotional. Mahler, too, had discovered music after gaining access to a relative's piano, in his case, his grandmother's, which he had found in her attic. Both were composers as well as conductors. Although Mahler spent most of his life in Europe, he had also come to the United States and served briefly in New York as conductor of the Philharmonic. And he, too, had not always had an easy time of it with the critics.

Mahler died in 1911, and for a long time his music remained relatively obscure. Others — Mitropoulos, for one — presented his music, but it was mainly Bernstein's attention, beginning in the 1960s, that propelled Mahler into a position of prominence.

As a result of Leonard Bernstein's own prominence, his birthday was sometimes honored with a large, public observance. In 1978, when he turned sixty, there was a memorable concert with the National Symphony Orchestra and an accompanying celebration at Wolf Trap, in Virginia.

As lovely as the occasion was, it came at a melancholy time in his life because Felicia had died of cancer only two months earlier. In its later years, their marriage had had its ups and downs, including a time of separation, but they were together at the end, and Bernstein was suffering for having lost her.

Twice more a milestone-birthday was marked by a major public celebration. In 1983, the site was Lawrence, Massachusetts, his birthplace. Members of his family, including his mother, accompanied him there. Bernstein took the opportunity to make a political statement by wearing a blue armband to symbolize hope for nuclear disarmament. Others, far and wide, joined him.

*Helping dismantle the Berlin Wall, December 1989*

In 1988, when he turned seventy, a gala celebration took place at Tanglewood, to honor both the man and the musician. Jamie wrote a song for the occasion and performed it, along with her husband David Thomas, her brother Alexander, and her sister Nina, on the stage of the Koussevitzky Music Shed, before a crowd of many thousand.

At seventy, Bernstein had become a much-beloved, highly revered senior statesman of music. Over the years, he had received many awards. In November 1989, three months after the celebration at Tanglewood, he was scheduled to receive another and very high one: the National Medal of the Arts. President Bush was to present it to him on November 17, in a ceremony at the White House, honoring the twelve recipients for 1989.

As the day drew near, Bernstein indicated that he was declining the award. He was protesting an action by the National Endowment for the Arts (NEA). In July, NEA had notified an arts organization in New York named Artists Space that it would receive a grant of $10,000 in support of an art exhibit about AIDS and its accompanying catalogue. But early in November, NEA impounded the funds. It did so out of apprehension that the award might be in violation of a directive from Congress not to provide support when the artwork was deemed to be obscene.

Bernstein was not alone in protesting. In fact, there was such a clamor from so many quarters that the chairman of the NEA finally restored the grant. Speculation then arose about whether Bernstein would receive the National Medal of the Arts after all. But it was no longer an option. Only twelve can be awarded. While the controversy over the grant to Artists Space was raging, a decision had been made on short notice to award a medal posthumously to Valdimir Horowitz, the magnificent pianist, who had very recently died.

Soon afterward, Bernstein's name was again in the news, linked to a political event. This one was much bigger and much happier. At midnight on November 9, 1989, East Germany had opened its borders, suddenly permitting its citizens to leave. They could even cross the Berlin Wall from East to West Berlin. Such splendid progress called for a musical celebration at the highest level. That could only mean one thing: the participation of Leonard Bernstein.

On the evening of December 23, he gave a concert in West Berlin. Then on Christmas morning, he repeated it in East Berlin. The music was Beethoven's Ninth Symphony, but Bernstein altered Schiller's accompanying words, substituting *"freiheit"* for *"freude."* Instead of an ode to joy, it became an ode to freedom.

Some especially important events were scheduled for the summer of 1990, and one was unprecedented. The Tanglewood Music Center, which Koussevitzky had begun in 1940, was observing its fiftieth anniversary. To celebrate, a tour had been planned for its orchestra, the first ever. It was going to Europe, and Bernstein was to lead it.

When he arrived at Tanglewood, it was obvious he was not well. Breathing was more of a chore than ever. He had to cancel some of his schedule, but on August 19, he managed to conduct part of a concert. No occasion could have been more appropriate as the final time he would ever conduct: it was the Koussevitzky Memorial Concert.

That evening he made a decision. He would not be able to accompany the Music Center Orchestra abroad. When the BSO subsequently cancelled the whole tour, the mood around Tanglewood was what one reporter described as "funereal."

Bernstein's own health deteriorated. On October 9, it was announced that he was retiring from conducting to concentrate his energy on composing. But his time was swiftly ending. Five days later, on October 14, in his home in New York, he died. Shortly thereafter, he was buried, next to Felicia, in a cemetary in Brooklyn.

On November 14, 1990, forty-seven years to the day after his spectacular debut in Carnegie Hall, a memorial concert was held there. Some of those closest to him spoke. In a spirit of gratitude for the life of her father, Jamie summed up very simply: "What fun we all had while it lasted." The final musical selection was the Overture to *Candide*, performed by the orchestra's players alone, facing an empty podium.

Some years earlier, he had addressed a gathering in Philadelphia at which he was being honored. His talk concluded:

All the world is a stage, with audiences searching for the perfect play. We may not reach perfection — this is not a utopian world — but all of us can strive toward that perfection. To do that: Keep rehearsing!

It was good advice. It had been offered by somone who understood it well.

The Maestro is dead. In America's heart, in all the world's heart, long live the Maestro!